GW00693749

EATING STRAW

THE NECR

MICHAEL HULSE, the son of an English father from the
Five Towns and a German mother from near Trier in the
Mosel valley, was born in 1955 and grew up in Stoke-on-
Trent. He studied German at the University of St
Andrews, and has subsequently taught English and
Commonwealth Literature at the universities of
Erlangen-Nürnberg, Eichstätt and Cologne in West
Germany, and has worked as a freelance writer and
translator in Durham, Oxford and Cologne. His reviews
of British, Commonwealth and German literature
appear in leading literary publications, and his work as a
translator includes Goethe's *The Sorrows of Young Werther*
and Jakob Wassermann's *Caspar Hauser* (both for
Penguin), as well as contemporary writing by Luise
Rinser, Botho Strauss and Elfriede Jelinek. His poetry
has earned him a number of awards; his other books are
Knowing and Forgetting (1981), *Propaganda* (1985) and
Mother of Battles (1991). Most recently he has co-edited
The New Poetry (1993), an anthology of work by more
than fifty of the younger British and Irish poets.

Michael Hulse

EATING
STRAWBERRIES
IN THE
NECROPOLIS

HARVILL
An Imprint of HarperCollins*Publishers*

First published in Great Britain in 1991
by Harvill
an imprint of HarperCollins*Publishers*,
77/85 Fulham Palace Road
Hammersmith, London w6 8jb

4 6 8 9 7 5 3

The author asserts the moral right to be
identified as the author of this work

A CIP catalogue record for this title
is available from the British Library

ISBN 0–00–272076–0

Printed and bound in Great Britain by
Hartnolls Limited, Bodmin, Cornwall

THIS BOOK IS FOR DORLE
AND FOR ALLEN

ACKNOWLEDGEMENTS

Most of these poems were first published in *Critical Quarterly*, *Encounter*, *Joe Soap's Canoe*, the *London Magazine*, the *London Review of Books*, *Other Poetry*, *Poetry Durham*, *Prospice*, *Stand*, *Thames Poetry* and the *Times Literary Supplement* in England; in *The Antigonish Review*, *Exile*, *Poetry Canada Review*, *Quarry* and *Waves* in Canada; and in *Poetry Australia* and *Quadrant* in Australia.

CONTENTS

Five Poems after Winslow Homer

EATING STRAWBERRIES IN
THE NECROPOLIS

Raffles Hotel

Singapore

Say a colonial sailed up the straits and saw
a fishing village. And set foot in a city.
    Say the future was opium
  traded for tea, parades on the padang,

secret societies, rickshaws on Collyer Quay,
and riots in the streets. Say an Armenian
    bought the villa where a bankrupt
  colonel had opened a tiffin parlour,

and made a white hotel, a place of colonnades
and frangipani, palms, pilasters, rattan blinds,
    piano waltzes in the court:
  the marriage of the bride to the roué.

And while men died at the Somme and at Passchendaele
a barman was (gently) shaking the first gin sling.
    While General Percival puffed
  and dallied, refusing to fortify

Singapore on the landward side, the Japanese
were riding down the peninsula on bikes. For
    history is a seduction:
  cocktails on the verandah, then dinner

at eight, and the stylish contempt of the waiters.
After the rain the sky is open again. Stars
    are holed in the indigo night.
  A British lord and lady lead their guests

to a private banquet where pipers are playing
"Scotland the Brave". An Australian swears that the
    last tiger killed on the island
  was shot underneath the billiard table.

This is the idiot empire. I'm lapping the
pool past midnight, thinking of Dad, and a jazz band's
    playing in the bar. After the
  war he dealt in textiles in Raffles Place,

and one day his driver came early to warn him
and hurry him to a villa where Englishmen
    waited armed behind shutters all
  the fanatical afternoon and night,

making light of their fears, but whispering, watching,
alert for a palm to sway as these do now, in
    the innocent air, trembling with
  the darker breathing of the saxophone.

A Chinese Tale

I dreamt I was the simple trusting boy
who took his wicked teacher's jealous hand
and climbed the mountain. And the teacher said
he had to go away, but he'd be back,
and if I happened to be hungry, why,
all I need do was eat the stones. His eyes
were fine strokes of a calligrapher's brush
conveying messages I could not read
(though how I longed to learn and understand).
I thanked the honest man for his advice
and said that I would wait till he returned.
He told me patience was a discipline
invaluable to a man. And left.

The day was bright, and I was young in hope,
and I questioned the sun, and the sun replied:
Study. Be humble. Be truthful. Aspire.
And I questioned the sky, and the sky replied:
Study. Be humble. Be truthful. Aspire.
And night came, and the ironic moon
replied with a smile: Be truthful. Aspire.
And keep up the studies. Because you know
that all will come to him who learns and waits.
But don't overdo the humility, boy.

And in the morning I was cold and hungry.

And I recalled the honest man's advice
and went about collecting stones, although

I must confess I'd never heard that stones
were good to eat. An inspiration came
and prompted me to warm them on my feet,
and in their place I saw a bowl of rice
and ate of it till I could eat no more.
And I questioned the sun, and the sun replied:
Study. Be humble. Be truthful. Aspire.
And I questioned the sky, and the sky replied:
Study. Be humble. Be truthful. Aspire.
And night came, and the ironic moon
replied with a smile: You're on the right track,
but remember that study's a means, not an end,
and aspiration's the vehicle, not the goal,
and humility may be counter-productive,
and even the truth isn't always the answer.

And in the morning I breakfasted on stones.

And the days went by, the days became weeks,
and, knowing that patience was a virtue
invaluable to a man, I waited,
hourly expecting my honest teacher's return.
And after forty days he did return,
important in his venerable robes,
and seemed surprised to find me still alive.
He listened with a serious expression
as I explained about the stones and rice.
The fine strokes narrowed into finer strokes.
I told him the sun's reply and he smiled.
I told him the sky's reply and he smiled.
I told him the moon's reply and he frowned.

And then it seemed I fell from off the mountain,
uncertain whether I was pushed, and woke

at daybreak on a square, where people cried
and ran and fell and lay where they had fallen.
And I questioned the rising sun and the sky
but they made no reply.
And I questioned the setting moon and the moon replied:
Today you died.

June 1989

Refugees

All night I've been driving this hearse of sleep
through dreams of dying, stunned by the dark,
and waking to the morning feel I've walked
into a photograph of war:
                                        across
the clods that litter a ploughed and stubborn field
three women come stumbling towards me,
a stooped old baggage in black and her daughters
struggling under the weight of refugee luggage,
picking an improvised footing through the furrows.
They're carrying too much. Their load's too cumbersome.
Sooner or later they'll have to leave something behind.
I watch them toil with their cases and basket,
negotiating a passage across the day
where minute after remembering minute
burns away like the farmhouse at their backs,
the smoke of the bombed-out past staining
the grey indifference of the heavens.
                                        Will
they walk right past? Without a word to me?
Where will they go? And will there be a season
when someone sees the seed green in the field?

The Architecture of Air

Though the waters still lap the ghat at Udaipur,
  the Minoan bull still leaps at Knossos,
Frederick's spirit still frets in Knobelsdorff's
  marble halls, and at Azay-le-Rideau
  bankers and kings contest the ghosting rights,

though stupefying superstructures of beauty
  still conform to the paradigms of power,
my lady paints an inch thick, my lord drives a Porsche,
  and fake apartment blocks line the approach
  to Termini when Hitler visits Rome,

our architect is still the architect of air,
  the making mouth, shaping the living breath:
teeth and tongue and lips, building a word or a kiss,
  expressing the inexpressible this.
  Whatever we say is said against death.

The gods are gone: in the Sistine ceiling a crack
  has come between Adam and creation,
the bombs explode in Belfast and Borobudur,
  Petra wears away to ignorant rock.
  Whatever we say is said against death.

Whatever we say is said against death. Adrift,
  listen you whisper, finger to your lips.
The oars shipped, the air unstirring, water dripping
  in stillness. And breathless we wait
  to hear each other say three simple words.

An American Murder

Where does the story begin? With the CBS crew
shooting footage for shocker shlock and slavering
    over their cameras as the
  bloodied Bostonian writhed in the driver's

seat by the gargling mess of his dying wife? Or half
an hour before, the Toyota pulled over, his
    finger cocked on the trigger, dull
  disbelief in the eyes of the horsy girl

he'd met at the Gourmet Club, the girl he'd installed in
a life of jacuzzis and pools and insurance?
    Somewhere in the nightmare there must
  be a dream. The dream that a man might have dreamt

who worked as the manager of a furrier store
on Newbury Street. The dream of a boy called Chuck.
    A boy who liked Paris, baseball,
  parties at Bill's. A boy who'd been to school at

the Immaculate Conception. The dream of a man
who'd check into the Sheraton Tara Hotel
    for his last night alive, a man
  who'd be hauled out of Boston harbour under

Tobin Bridge the next morning, leaving a letter on
Tara paper expressing regret for the
    trouble he'd caused everybody
  and saying he couldn't go on. The trouble?

No more than the usual trouble. The usual niggers
arrested. The usual panic in Boston's
        suburbs where whites could understand
    a man who would fill his house with foodie books.

No more than the usual Ave Maria and
tears at the funeral when Chuck's farewell was read,
        beginning *Goodnight, sweet wife*. No
    more than the usual murder. And after

the killing and lying he went to an agent's and
booked a Winter Getaway, never supposing
        that winter was forever and
    was colder than he'd believed in his coldest dreams.

Fornicating and Reading the Papers

John Stubbs of Lincoln's Inn has written a pamphlet:
   The Discoverie of a Gaping Gulf
to swallow England by a French Marriage.
   The queen has seen the pamphlet, at least
the title page. She is burning with choler.
   She says this Stubbs is a seditious villain.

This is the stage set up in the market place
   at Westminster. This is seditious Stubbs.
This is the butcher's knife, keen against his wrist.
   This is the mallet that strikes against the knife.
The moment his right hand is off, seditious Stubbs
   doffs his hat with his left, crying *God save the queen*!

II

Wet from the shower
   towelling your breasts
you ask me if I've read
   Motley's *Rise of the Dutch Republic.*

My heart is in another question: *What*
   is the price of a virtuous woman?
Ads in the London Underground reply:
   Buy her a diamond before someone else does.

III

The Sudanese minister shrugs. *It is only a hand,*
   he declares, *a small price to pay*
for the preservation of law and order.
   The minister drums his fingers on the desk.

This is the guilty man, whose hand
   was found in another man's pocket.
He watches the amputation carefully.
   No noble words are waiting in his mouth,
no thoughts of God or saving in his head.

   His hand is preserved in a jar of surgical alcohol.

IV

A dusty lane
   in the polder
the flat
   loveliness
and the high
   cloud-shattered sky
caressed by alders
   the room where we lay
shuttered against the day
   breathing
the white smell
   of apples in the loft
the fragrance of grass
   the touch of it:

for days I was whistling
   those bars from the rondo
movement of Beethoven's first
   piano concerto.

V

He is a missionary. From Detroit.
   They, the Sendero Luminoso, know
that he is the CIA. America made flesh.
   Into that flesh they drive needles, beneath
the toenails. One of his eyes has been pulped
   by a rifle-butt. They have crushed his testicles.

They know what they know. They are the gods
   on the shining path of righteousness.
Now they hack off his fingers one by one.
   Unable to give the answers they require,
My God, why hast thou he breathes, and
   passes out again, till the pain revives him.

VI

María said to Yerma
   Haven't you held
a living bird in your hand?
   well that's what it's like,
having a child inside,
   only more in the blood.

Nine Points of the Nation

I

Living on this island in the
    American sphere of influence, where
the crappy drollery of history
    crackles across the daily air
reminding us that boredom is
    banal and for ridiculous reasons
will re-elect the ill-intentioned,
    you'll learn a yearning for exile.

II

After they sealed
    the airfield off
with seven miles
    of razor wire,
they counted the cost:
    the several millions
of pounds, the pulse-
    beat of fear.

III

The head of our government likes
    to be photographed with children.

IV

Syntax gone rigid in the mouth.
    A seven-year-old hanged at Norwich
for stealing a petticoat. Crows crying *dirt*!
    Your work will set you free.

V

Beautiful Old York paving stones,
    rectangular, in good
condition, ex-public footpath.
    Offered at £80 per ton
plus VAT including carriage.
    Free genuine Victorian street lamp
complete, worth £300,
    with every order of 16 tons or more.

VI

Pepys came on Lady Sandwich "doing
    something upon the pot" in the dining-room.

VII

Here at Tyburn Tree we sit
    in Mother Proctor's Pews.
The nation's full of public shit.
    This is the six o'clock news.

VIII

I've never liked this city, not
   compared with Vienna, say, or Amsterdam.
It has a small and smutty atmosphere,
   the cramped crush of a city that has got
and spent: a truthless tract written
   in stale legitimation of Britain.
I visit and choke on the pride.
   That mighty heart is lying, still!

IX

Come out from the dark, my love, we'll ride to where
   the Underground comes up for light and air.

1985

Snakes

The afternoon was peppery with the smells
of the vines, insecticide, red earth and shale
as we walked up the vineyard past the blasted
concrete shell of a pillbox that overlooked
      the valley. A buzzard
turned like a kite at the end of a cord and a lizard
      lay on a blood-hot rock
pulsing with luxury in the knot of heat.

As we came out on the road past the trees, Dad
glimpsed a wriggle and held me by the shoulder.
Don't move. We watched a flimsy twist of fabric
jag across the laborious tarmac. *He'll*
      be more afraid of you
than you are of him, if he notices you said Dad. And
      we watched the adder twitch
to the verge where grass began and disappear.

It had hardly occurred to me to be scared.
Of eighteen inches of rope? A snake was the
cobra that terrified you in the bathroom
in Kipling's story "Rikki Tikki Tavi"
      which Dad had read to me
last winter by the fireside. A snake was the thirty-foot
      anaconda in a
nature book I had. And Sister Augustine

had even claimed that there was a snake in the
Garden of Eden (she didn't say what kind).
This gave the whole business a sinister twist:
India and Brazil were faraway places,
        but I played in gardens
myself, and who could tell when a Wagler's pit viper would
        spit from the bushes as
I searched for a cricket ball knocked for a six?

Last year when I drove the gently sloping miles
from Carmona down to the Guadalquivir
I thought of that moment with Dad when I stopped
by the roadside to buy some oranges. In
        the dust lay an adder
a car had caught, its jaws a crimson ochre, gaping, gashed
        behind the arrowhead:
the Garden's defender. Beautiful. And dead.

Roadworkers Picking Cherries

The first, wearing rumpled cords belted with clothes–line,
   climbs on the wall where the shade crumples and
flaps, and takes off the hat that reminds him of the
   wine he drank sitting under a fig tree
in a Sicilian village. The straw is frayed
   and feathering at the crown, but he holds
the hat in a pinch of affection, the fonder
   of it the more it weathers, and fans the
air to cool his face. From the fields the laughter of
   children. The fragrance of hay. He reaches
up to the dark blood-coloured cherries and plucks and
   drops a fruit in his hat, then another,
and goes on picking, contented, feeling the warmth
   of the afternoon. It is good. His hat
is filling.
        The younger man in blue overalls
   is thinking how peaceful the silence is
now they've switched off the generator.
                     Soon there are
   five of them up on the wall, picking and
laughing and spitting the stones in the orchard grass,
   and the man with the hat has eaten through
to the base of the crown, which is stained with juice, and
   he sits at the dusty roadside, and pulls
the brim of his hat to shadow his brow, hearing
   the single excitement of a lark and
knowing the dark red stains in his hat will forever
   recall a day when he sat with the taste
of cherries in his mouth and looked out on the fields
   fading to pale blue in the distant hills.

To Gottlob Fabian

died at Tarnast, 4 March 1844

In Vormärz Brandenburg
six iron generations back
across the blood and soil
you worked a windmill at Tarnast.

I know your stolid windmill,
gentle and firm, wooden and white,
set on the flats of Brandenburg,
tenderly taking the wind.

I know the stones, the stones that grind,
the principle of what is fine.
I know your watchfulness, your eye,
your patience, and your sky:

we are sails of the same windmill
stilled, tensed to a nameless, windstill
breathing culled from the very air,
again becoming air.

Sundown, Landing the Catch

Pangandaran, Java

Light silvers
the shivering sand.
Steady waters
beat to the land,

and fishermen leap in the waves to beach
their red and blue trimaran,
bringing home the daily catch
to Pangandaran,

bringing the daily hopes.
Their women are hauling
hand over hand at the ropes,
toiling.

The sun is a fanned
braiding.
The fishermen stand on the sand
in a shifting fading.

In a year they can earn as much,
if they're in luck,
as I who watch
can earn in a week:

how can that be just?
The question is ash.
The question is dust.
The sun is a golden coin. The sun is cash.

The Parable of the Blind

In the kitchen courtyard sunlight
strikes off the cooling cauldron of bright
water and off the blade of the axe.

The black-haired sad Armenian
is singing and splitting the shining
wood with his shining axe:

Ruschuk! Ruschuk! Ruschuk! –
the clean sound of our town
chopped sharp and clear,

fear and love and sadness shining
bright in his singing as his axe
rises and falls, rises and falls.

The past is all an unforgetting
witnessing: his sister killed
before his eyes in Istanbul.

Now a clear-eyed Ruschuk boy
watches from childhood's window as
the sharp Armenian

tenses, terrible, in the bright
burning heart of the yard, and brings
his axe down hard on the loving past.

The Baby Killer

If you have understood how a boy will run
with an orange in his hand or a pomegranate,
understood in your blood and in your loins,
you know how he will run when he kills a man.

Look, in the shade. You see what the kids have drawn
on the road, in chalk? The outline of a man.
That's how police record where a body lay.
Palermo is a city of guilty games.

You must not be surprised. It does not come
from television. That is for innocents.
The children play at murders they have seen.
And then before too long they kill for real.

We call them baby killers. Shall we sit here,
out of the sun? This heat is punishing,
and in the corner we shall be more private.
A Ramazotti for myself, perhaps.

Murder is cheap in Sicily. And boys
under fourteen come at the price you'd pay
for a weekend in a modest hotel in Rome.
You mustn't think supply is ever short.

As you know, when we go to church we remove
the radios from our cars and take them with us.
A sensible precaution. So Damiano
was bending over, fitting the radio back.

My brother must have heard the boy call out,
asking the time or shouting abuse, who knows,
and turned. He took four bullets in the chest.
A boy was seen, running, but never found.

Elena walked with me in the orange groves.
She said she couldn't sleep. I said I'd lost
a brother but I still had Sicily.
She said she could not lie with Sicily.

You can imagine how a boy will run
when he kills a man. You know it in your blood.
You know he is running into a hungry future.
He wants to live. And be his murdered man.

I told Elena I could learn to love
the subtle beauty of a killer's gun.
She spat. I wiped my face and turned away.
She called me back. But I began to run.

Horns

Look at Buonarotti's pasta-bearded Moses
slouching like a boxer resting in his corner.

A patriarchal bully-boy.
Mister Universal Law.
With beefy biceps, bodybuilder thighs,
and features modelled on the Pope.
A bruiser of the soul. *With horns.*

Not the fault of Michelangelo.

A mistranslation does the work
of fifty vicars. Exodus
declares that coming down from Sinai
Moses shone. The Vulgate gave him horns.

And every Sunday morning
sexton Jägle crossed the grass
beneath the sycamores
to ask the numbers of the hymns
Herr Schweitzer wanted sung,
and paused to rub a thoughtful thumb
across young Albert's temples, grunting:
Yes, the horns are growing.

The boy heard piping in the forest. And
his cloven-footed fear
went walking on the mountain.

Dalí in the Torre Galatea

I might as well be a mannequin.
Is this silk I'm wearing? Death will be silly.

Mornings they lift me from the bed to the chair.
I might as well be sitting in a Cadillac.

Arturo used to drive me. Now he shaves me.
Maria Teresa reads the papers to me.

I might as well be a clever fake of myself.
They feed me through a tube up my nose.

The wall outside my window looks like Greta Garbo's lips.
I might as well be dead.

You'd think I was a bathtub. Or a snail.
Is this air I'm breathing? Living is silly.

You'd think I was alive.
I might as well be alive.

1987

Concentrating

Standing at the
window watching

three Italian
women rowing,

rocking and tipping and
bobbing, I hear

their laughter find
its natural level

like water. Stay.
Take a look.

Don't you agree,
the flyaway girl

in the cherry cloche
looks like Zelda Fitzgerald?

I'd wave to her
but both my hands

are occupied
unbuttoning your blouse.

Carnation, Lily, Lily, Rose

after John Singer Sargent

Of the several answers to darkness, better than sleep
and lovelier is the lighting of lanterns in gardens,
the claustrophiliac revelation of closeness, light
laden with intimate comfort: important harmony!
      Two girls in white

inhabit this acquiescent tenderness, Alices
cool in Marian shifts, innocents lavender-scented
and cotton-stockinged – you think of Betjeman's bicycle-
riding Oxford girls, the avuncular arousal these
      slim-limbed little

women trigger. What kind of Eden *is* this, anyway,
where only emblematic flowers grow? – carnations for the
experience of blood, lilies for virginity, and
roses modest and flushed (Lolitadom of girlhood!) like
      laundered bloodstained

linen. They are not girls but ideas of girls, and in
the otherworld of intimate green already their thoughts
are of leaving their paradise, as women in Watteau
dream of flying: see, it is in their serious faces
      taking the glow.

Voyeurs

The city was my lover. And the light
fell from the shoulders of the afternoon.

Two women on a balcony
that August evening, leaning
on the Empire ironwork and watching
workmen walking homeward in the dusk.
Imagining the smell of work and musk.

And there was Paul the poet with his notebook,
adding *asphodèles* to rhyme with *hirondelles*,
imagining the bed they might have left.

I watched them all, the women and the poet,
then watched the swallows in the air
and wondered if the swallows felt
the tenderness of Paris.

Behind me in a naked field
of grass and asphodel and sage
you waited with impatient country love
and asked me would I fucking use my pen
or was I only talk like other men.

I walked into the valley of the page.

At Avila

A poet's distributing photocopied verse
for a few pesetas and a pathetic boy
    tries begging from the woman who
    pulled up in the Porsche in a squall of dust

and now sits testily scanning *La Revista*,
sunglasses cocked in her mane and a pendent breast
    relaxing out of her T-shirt
    whenever she leans for an olive. Me,

I'm watching her over the top of a battered
Penguin Classics *Life of Saint Teresa*, drinking
    an Aguila beer and thinking
    of Teresa's image of the waters –

the difficult and laborious water drawn
from a well, the water moved by a water-wheel,
    the water that flows in a stream,
    and the water that falls from heaven: rain.

The boy's getting nowhere. The woman's ignoring
his mute imploring stare, and she raises her arms
    to stretch, and her flesh lifts as well
    and strains at her shirt, and my denim strains

and pulses for passion in the barren garden.
I return to Teresa's water. What did it
    really mean? That while her spirit
    was busy with God, her body was hot

for a fuck? What of it? I watch as the woman
purses her glistening lips to spit out a pit.
    The boy moves on. To me. I give.
    Graceless and hasty, I give to be rid

of his presence at my pleasures here in the shade
of a cool arcade on the Plaza de Santa
    Teresa. I give, and the boy
    bows with contemptuous gratitude, and

the woman runs a deliberate hand inside
her T-shirt, smiling, like an accomplice in sin.
    If God (wrote Teresa) *withholds*
    the water of grace, no work is enough.

Eating Strawberries in the Necropolis

Suppose I had ridden
naked in the Garden in the cavalcade of men
astride a sardonic gryphon, driving the roads
that wove among the dusty olive groves
and coming out on the final commanding miles
across the straight to Carmona, my companions
jouncing on leopards and dromedaries and stallions,
chimaeras and unicorns, into an afternoon sun
hung low on the blinding horizon, under
the hieratic frown of stork and peacock,
metallic dazzles flashing off the trucks,
my thighs hot on the creature's flanks
as I drove the Roman road to the rock
where Man had watched, lord of the wilderness.

Suppose I had ridden
naked all night in the Garden of Delights,
ridden around the water where the women
parleyed with ravens and egrets, ridden
till morning stood like a tree at the window.
And, waking, wanted you.

What else would I do
but walk to the poppied necropolis and sit
on a wall in the shade of the cypresses,
eating strawberries from a paper bag.

The flesh was tender, red as cactusflower.
The juices bled to stain the imperial dust.

Adultery

There's my presbyterian attitude
to deal with, and your honest heart.

I have been lying here, my cheek
against your breast, remembering

a French corvette that lay on Lake
Ontario, grey in the bright

of a starry night, fingers of light
unclenching tenderly across

the black and fractured gentleness of water.
Hold me. Every love has the government it

deserves. Our parliament is hung,
our members are corrupt.

You didn't warm your instrument
you told your gynaecologist, he said

I did my best, you said
Be gentle, I'm upset. My husband

wants to have children, I don't think I even
love him. I remember

two men looking into a station wagon:
Isn't she a dandy? In the back

a dead doe, bundled on a sheet of plastic,
lay in sticky blood, her belly slit.

II

No guarantees. No promises. No hope.
In the long run I'll do what's best for me.

You talk about your island at Parry Sound
and swimming naked in the sheath of cold,

about the Tina Turner wig
you bought on Yonge at Hallowe'en.

All talk. *I need you. Hold me.* Every love
could do with a reminder of Colbert:

picture us in the forest of Tronçais,
where oaks grown straight three hundred years

thrash their crowns in the topmost air,
each one intended for a mast.

What you see dappling the earth with shade
is the sadness of the rational dream,

the pathos and the pity of the past:
the oaks were planted in 1670 and

matured in the nineteenth century,
when shipping changed to steam.

An Aluminium Casket Would
Be a Good Idea

My friend Deedee, who is clever and bitter, whose
husband paddled away one day in a canoe,

said she is only having female pallbearers
(dressed, she thinks, in Anne Klein black).

Shelda said there were too many stairs
at Lady of Sorrows, so Deedee said

it could be at All Saints
and Shelda said there was no parking.

I dreamt of my first husband last night.
First time ever. He had put on too much weight

and wanted to give our marriage another try.
I was revolted, but for some reason

he seemed to be living in the same house.
I don't like myself right now. Slack.

Women don't like getting older.
They switch to 15 watt bulbs

(I need a flashlight to get around in here),
wear gloves so they don't look at their hands

on the steering wheel, and stop using
the rear view mirror so they don't catch

a glimpse of themselves. I told Deedee
an aluminium casket

would be a good idea. Karen said
Why don't you just go out and get

yourself a horse, and forget everything.
We drank too much wine, and watched

Anne of Green Gables, a beautiful TV
production, we were all weeping and

a little drunk. All I have ever wanted
for anyone is happiness. And my freedom.

II

Most of it you probably can guess.
My father used to listen to the news

on CFRB, usually in the driveway in his car.
He was so much like clockwork

he would arrive home at 5.50
and listen to the news before getting out

of his car. My father was strict, small,
he used to work out the horses at

the racetrack as a kid. He had his own
car dealership, and sold it at the right time,

and got into boats, bringing up
the slickcraft from Chicago. I was his.

I foxhunted with him and went to horse shows
and won the occasional ribbon. He kept

an eye on me all the time.
I went to private school, wore a kilt,

was a prefect and drove a yellow Triumph
convertible and was hard on the boys I dated.

He didn't much approve of either marriage.
Just before my father became a

management problem (wandering, pissing)
we took him for an assessment.

He couldn't name my children or make small change.
He knew the prime minister, though;

even at his worst he had political views.
Then he got sick, Alzheimer's, and lost his mind.

I love you now. I dreamt of you.
I was trying to clean myself with wet toilet paper

and it was spit-balling all over the place,
and I heard you pick up some keys

and I thought you were leaving the room
so I dashed out not worrying about anything.

Easter Sunday Deedee sat on a rock
for five whole hours and did not call

her rat of an awful father, for the first time in her life.
Just sat there.

III

Jack tore the fucking fireplace apart
last week for a cool $1000

to fix a smoking problem and has now
created the smoking problem on the second floor.

Do you know, I can have most things I want *if I ask*.
Just like being with my father. Dollar by dollar.

In the long run Jack has always done either
what is right or what I've wanted.

His mother is a monarchist. She lives
in her husband's family home, and has never been

more than fifteen miles from Collingwood.
The family home was built in 1890.

The curtains have hung since 1890.
It's truly original. Stains and all.

Pictures of the Queen, and Winston Churchill.
The Illustrated London News.

Multicoloured towels in the upstairs bathroom.
Bathtub peeling so badly you're scared of lockjaw.

Jack was furious, frightened, wouldn't
allow me to have the child. I was in

my thirteenth week when I found out I was pregnant.
I went to Hampstead, New York. A cattle line-up.

The doctor prodded me carelessly.
This one's saline. I said *Forget it.*

He said okay, he'd do a D & C,
and of course it wasn't complete, I was too far.

They couldn't stop the bleeding.
Does our life only teach us to think things through

and act responsibly? When I came back
from Belgium, I brought some Gueuze for Jack,

it double ferments, he wouldn't drink it
because it was milky. All the time the cork

kept trying to come out on the plane.

The Evidence of Things not Seen

Georgian Bay, Ontario

Jagged jack-pine characters
snagged like battered parasols

building unbuilding in the shimmering
shining westward on the lake:

There's nothing there. Examining
the weaving air: *We're always getting*

ready to live, but never living.
Happiness. The beautiful illusions.

And love has shot a shuttle
through the weft of light and water,

holding close as faith:
living further into the fertile

shifting of the shaping air,
certain of everything we haven't seen.

To Botho Strauss in Berlin

Your cool high-ceilinged life
is naked as a stage,

as if you'd taken an apartment where
the set-designer of your dreams

had recently moved out.
It is a theatre after the première,

filled up to emptiness with applause.
I think of God the Almighty after the ball,

sitting as you imagined him
on the palace steps, asleep in his slippers and topper.

Let there (he mumbles in his slumber,
dreamy and calmly afraid) *be light*.

The Country of Pain and Revelation

The woman sitting on the glinting barrier
watching a stir of air relentlessly uplift
   the silver undersides of leaves
  is breathing very carefully, as if

afraid that she might be too tender for breathing.
Her hand is resting in the dusty hair of the
   man lying jack-knifed on the grass
  between the glittering strips of metal

that run down the centre reserve. She does not see
the slowed traffic, the flashing lights approaching. She
   is elsewhere. Again the country
  of pain and revelation has a guest.

Again the great light has ground the peaks to powder.
Again in the valleys the shadows have sheltered
   the traveller standing alert
  at the rail of the ferry, the trader

bargaining with the goatherd, and the trapper, still
and meticulous in his secretive sidelight.
   It is the discovered country
  from which, returning in wonder as if

from memories of the dreams we thought forgotten,
we sunder in awe, wanting. What is the meaning
   of graining in a rockface? What
  annunciation hides in a hut built

high on an outcrop overlooking the nowhere,
bared to the higher nowhere of the air? And why must
    we find that after our truest
  transmigrations, after our fertile hopes,

we still are left with smashed metal and glass, resting
fingers in the hair of a dying lover? She
    knows the name of the place. Leaning
  forward, she kisses the dusty lips and

cradles his head and places her cheek against his,
and he learns to say yes, say yes, and goes home to
    a lighted house, a dazzle of
  horror, security, darkness and love.

Five Poems after Winslow Homer

for Christopher Koch

I · LONG BRANCH, NEW JERSEY
1869

A northern reconstructionist parade
of confidence and crinolines! as if
    a midday promenade
    on the crest of a sunlit cliff

were equal to the knowledge that dispels
our doubts of an experience of grace:
    the shopgirls and the belles,
    in cotton and velvet and lace,

pursuing their quest for first causes, stop
before oblivion's pavilion
    to review from the top
    the proven conclusions of sun –

each one of them a fresh hypothesis
of flesh, bundled and tucked into bustles
    and berthas. Their hair is
    bobbed and they carry parasols;

see, here are love and vanity and grief,
attested in the rhetoric of light,
    a statement of belief
    said like a charm against the night.

II · A BASKET OF CLAMS
1873

Me and my cousin Toby
are walking across the sands
one hand each on the handle
of a basket full of clams.

We've rolled our pants up to the knee
my cousin Toby and me
cos we've been down to fetch the clams
from down at the sea.

There's boats here high up in the dry
and dead fish on the beach
my house is just a short way back
out of the ocean's reach.

My pa says God's in everything
he says we're grains of sand
tickling sharp between God's toes
or held in God's great hand.

My pa says God's in the biggest whale
and the smallest fish that swam
He's in a dogfish and a cod
and even in a clam.

So me and my cousin Toby
are walking across the sands
one hand each on the handle
of a basket full of clams.

III · HUNTER IN THE ADIRONDACKS
1892

Because
   and only because
I know
   the way I mean to go, I'll pause
here in the forest underglow
   and listening and looking stand
gun in hand
   at one with the natural laws
I understand.

   What is a man that spends his life in lying?

These are the forests of the Adirondacks:
   the simple imperatives guide my feet
among the praising birches and maples and pines,
   the rusty russets of rotting timbers,
the greens of growing, the golds of dying.
   I know this country like the lines in my hand.
I know the directions, I know the names and numbers.
   I have my trapping wire. My gun. My axe.
I shall survive. I can read the signs.
   I know the self I need to meet.

This is no land
   for theophobiacs.

IV · THE FOX HUNT
1893

Slow
slurred dead–downdragging
faltering floundering step in the deep snow,
strength failing, will flagging,

numbing night
drawing a darkness over the cold white:
a painted fox,
pounding with panic's

pulsebeat bursting in all the important blood,
about to die at the moment of creation.
The fox demands to know the god
of paint and canvas, the god

of the printed page now thirteen lines complete –
but Death is battering
blackly across the immediate
blankness of the moment, the beat of a wing

tears the air with godlike savagery,
impatient of paint. Where is the need
for the fox to die in the snow? we
ask; but berries emblematically bleed,

the crows are cruel, the poem nearly done,
and we know that the real fox, caught
in a greedy creator's grasp, tormented and torn,
will disappear into art, into the death of thought.

V · KISSING THE MOON
1904

I

Steadily the salt weed stench,
evil dead sea smell,
fetor of the greedy trench,
deep reek of the swell,

fills the breathing head with fear's
seeping seagreen taint,
reaching past the feral years
from Homer's fathomed paint:

fear breeds, breeds like the ocean's
miseries and joys.
On our terror's tidal motions
ride derisive buoys,

pointing to the hostile rocks
where our hopes went down;
teach me one more paradox,
darling, and I drown.

Teach me Christ is risen for love.
Teach me God is dead.
Teach me of the fiery dove.
Teach me to forget.

Onward into night we row,
three men in an Ark:
though the little that we know
brightens the deep dark,

still the light the spirit craves
bides invisible.
At the mercy of the waves,
but closer every pull,

breasting crests of wise desires,
westward we return.
Far to east we see her rise,
cold and kindly moon,

full and virginal and white,
kissed by the fool foam:
we are on a godless tide,
rowing home.

To Allen Curnow

Late light on the lake
and the ferry's wake is
filled with a silver

shiver: yes, the world
can end any time it likes
and that will be all (I

suppose) but first you'll
pull at your pipe and tell
another story, happily,

wrinkling your eyes
in concentrated quiet
and crinkling your contented face

like the man who has drawn out
Leviathan: your talking
is like walking with a friend

in gentle country where at last
beyond a rough stone wall
we come upon the sea

but when you write
you trust to the great water
and take your passage on

the ferry's element as if
the open white of a wake
need never close again.

NOTES

Though Dalí, Botho Strauss and Allen Curnow will need no introduction, one name in the book will certainly be unfamiliar, that of Gottlob Fabian. He was one of my German forefathers, the remotest I am aware of. Since the poem written to him deliberately moves upon sensitive territory, I should state that my awareness of his existence comes from an *Ahnenpass* (Third Reich documentation of "Aryan" ancestry) which until her death was in my maternal grandmother's possession. Some of my other sources ought to be mentioned. In "An American Murder" I have helped myself to details of the Stuart murder case as reported in the *Independent* (13 January 1990). Charles Stuart shot his pregnant wife in the head and himself in the groin, invented a black assailant, stood by as a black suspect was arrested for the murder, collected a first insurance pay-off, began to make new plans, and finally killed himself, when his brother revealed the facts of the case. Two other poems in the book draw on newspaper reports. "The Parable of the Blind" uses a passage in Elias Canetti's *Die Gerettete Zunge* (*The Tongue Set Free*). "Voyeurs" is a response to Verlaine's "Les amies: sur le balcon". In the series of poems on the loss of faith, written after paintings by the American artist Winslow Homer (1836–1910), I have twice used structural models: "The Fox Hunt" follows Ted Hughes's "The Thought-Fox", and "Kissing the Moon" follows the later version of Goethe's "An den Mond". "To Allen Curnow" owes everything to his poem "A Reliable Service".

Poetry in Harvill Paperbacks

ANNA AKHMATOVA

Selected Poems
Translated from the Russian by Stanley Kunitz with Max Hayward

RAYMOND CARVER

A New Path to the Waterfall
Last Poems

PAUL DURCAN

A Snail in My Prime
New and selected Poems

HOMER

The Odyssey
Translated from the Ancient Greek by Robert Fitzgerald

JAAN KAPLINSKI

The Same Sea in Us All
Translated from the Estonian by the author with Sam Hamill

JAAN KAPLINSKI

The Wandering Border
Translated from the Estonian by the author
with Sam Hamill and Riina Tamm

ALEKSANDR KUSHNER

Apollo in the Snow
Selected Poems 1960–1987
Translated from the Russian by Paul Graves and Carol Ueland

OSIP MANDELSTAM

Stone
Translated from the Russian by Robert Tracy

BORIS PASTERNAK

Poems 1955–1959 with *An Essay in Autobiography*
Translated from the Russian by Michael Harari and Manya Harari

VIRGIL

The Aeneid
Translated from the Latin by Robert Fitzgerald